What Happens

When You Die

Michael W. Newman

What Happens When You Die
Published by CreateSpace Publishing
A division of Amazon.com

©2011 Michael W. Newman

Printed in the United States of America

For information:
www.mnewman.org

Dedication:

To the saints--our friends and loved ones who have been carried into the presence of Jesus before us.

Contents

Questions About Death

There was a rich man who was dressed in purple and fine linen and lived in luxury every day. At his gate was laid a beggar named Lazarus, covered with sores and longing to eat what fell from the rich man's table. Even the dogs came and licked his sores.

The time came when the beggar died and the angels carried him to Abraham's side. The rich man also died and was buried. In hell, where he was in torment, he looked up and saw Abraham far away, with Lazarus by his side. So he called to him, "Father Abraham, have pity on me and send Lazarus to dip the tip of his finger in water and cool my tongue, because I am in agony in this fire."

But Abraham replied, "Son, remember that in your lifetime you received your good things, while Lazarus received bad things, but now he is comforted here and you are in agony. And besides all this, between us and you a great chasm has been fixed, so that those who want to go from here to you cannot, nor can anyone cross over from there to us."

He answered, "Then I beg you, father, send Lazarus to my father's house, for I have five brothers. Let him warn them, so that they will not also come to this place of torment."

Abraham replied, "They have Moses and the Prophets; let them listen to them."

"No, father Abraham," he said, "but if someone from the dead goes to them, they will repent."

He said to him, "If they do not listen to Moses and the Prophets, they will not be convinced even if someone rises from the dead" (Luke 16:19-31).

One
Questions About Death

+

"It's toughest at night."

That's what the widower told me just weeks after his wife of more than 50 years died. His eyes welled up with tears. This was the most difficult challenge he ever faced. Now he had a myriad of questions:

- Was she all right?

- Where was she now?

- Did she remember him?

- What did she look like?

- What was she doing?

- Will I see her again?

- Will she know me?

Facing death can be gut wrenching.

I have walked the journey of grief with people who have suffered because of the death of friends, brothers, sisters, parents, spouses, and children. I've lived through it, too. Not long after I completed this book draft, my wife's most precious friend died prematurely and tragically. She and my wife shared years of growing up together. They took walks in the country, rescued turtles from harm, split slices of pizza, experienced harrowing teenage adventures, laughed, cried, and prayed together. In an instant, just four days after Christmas, she was gone. With the sobs and heartbreaking hurt came questions.

The questions came from deep within. Just like the experience of every person who has suffered grief and loss, the questions grew out of a heart that cared deeply about a precious person who had died.

It is important to realize that questions about the afterlife do not usually grow out of simple intellectual curiosity or idle theological musing. It is true that the subject comes up in the context of seeking knowledge. But the deep and desperate questions about what happens when you die frequently grow out of a profound longing for a loved one. They are desperate cries from the heart and soul, wanting to know that this isn't the end. They are questions that crave more than information. They crave hope. At one point eternity is an afterthought, a distant idea for the future. Suddenly it is a new and urgent reality, the only reality that can bring comfort and answers.

I've asked these questions about people I have loved. Losing someone close to you changes your perspective. You wonder why it happened. You wrestle with the connection between now and eternity. You look forward to the reunion ahead. You hope your loved one is safe, healthy, and fulfilled.

Unfortunately, in an effort to offer consolation to the grieving, well-intentioned people have offered some confusing takes on what happens when someone dies. I've heard talk about loved ones turning into angels. Theories are offered about people entering a deep sleep after death.

But what does the Bible say about what happens when you die? Does God give any answers?

In the middle of this search for answers, I read Jesus' words in Luke chapter 16. Jesus was telling a story about a rich man and a poor beggar named Lazarus. In verse thirteen Jesus introduced the conversation:

> *"No servant can serve two masters. Either he will hate the one and love the other, or he will be devoted to the one and despise the other. You cannot serve both God and money."*

The Pharisees responded to this statement by sneering at Jesus. Jesus' reaction was to hammer the point home with a story. In verse nineteen Jesus began the parable of the rich man and Lazarus. Jesus' main point, of course, was that riches could very well become a stumbling block to salvation. Money may even deceive the possessor into believing that he has everything—including favor with God.

But there is something else compelling about this parable. In the process of telling this powerful story to teach His listeners about money and priorities, Jesus pulled the curtain back to reveal details about the afterlife. In a matter-of-fact way Jesus gave clear answers about what happens when a believer or unbeliever dies.

And why wouldn't He? Why wouldn't the Son of God give answers about what every child of God will face? Every one of us will experience the end of this life. Either we will die or we will see Jesus come back and put a stop to the broken course of this world. We may try to deny that eternity is coming. Our culture may mask, sanitize, and try to tame the fact of death. But no one will escape the inevitable. This life will end. Eternity will be ushered in.

So, why wouldn't Jesus be open about life everlasting? Why would He keep the afterlife a total mystery when life with Him forever is what He wants us to yearn for?

This book will take a close look at Jesus' words and provide His answers for the questions grieving and searching people ask. My prayer is that you will listen closely to the One who knows the truth about what happens when you die and that the words of Jesus will direct you, encourage you, strengthen your faith, fill you with hope, and give you endurance and purpose until that great day when our Lord Jesus meets us face to face.

Chapter One Questions for Thought and Discussion

1. What are some of the questions you have about what happens after you die?

2. Which questions puzzle you most or don't have answers that satisfy you?

3. How might answers help bring strength during grief?

4. Read 1 Thessalonians 4:13. What does this verse say about the knowledge God desires you to have as you face grief and death?

5. What does it mean to "grieve like the rest of men, who have no hope"?

6. Who in your life needs the knowledge and comfort God wants to provide? Name at least one person who might be blessed by what you learn in this study.

7. Read Psalm 23. What knowledge and comfort about life, death, and the afterlife do these verses provide? Talk about how this Psalm impacts your life.

Verse of Comfort: Psalm 23:6 *"Surely goodness and love will follow me all the days of my life, and I will dwell in the house of the Lord forever."*

Note the names of loved ones you are remembering as you read this book:

Where Are You After You die?

"The time came when the beggar died and the angels carried him to Abraham's side. The rich man also died and was buried. In hell, where he was in torment..."

Two
Where Are You After You Die?

+

What happens when someone dies? Do people drift into a long "soul sleep" as they wait for the resurrection of the dead on the Last Day? Is there a holding area until the end comes? Do people have to wait for the rest of the world to catch up? Not according to Jesus. When Lazarus died, the angels carried him to Abraham's side. Lazarus went to heaven right away.

Picture poor Lazarus lying in the street. He was a crumpled heap at the gate of the rich man's house. Unshowered, filthy, smelly, and undesirable, he strained to receive sustenance from passers by, from the rich man's servants as they came and went, and from the rich man himself. Perhaps, in the quiet of the early morning or late evening, Lazarus overheard conversations coming from the rich man's home. Through the open windows the poor beggar may have even heard the steady and rhythmic reading of the Torah—the utterance of the Word of God drifting into the street and falling gently onto the hopeless man's ears. In the midst of his torment, Lazarus must have trusted in the Redeemer and Savior revealed in Holy Writ. When he died, he joined the Shepherd of his soul. Lazarus went to heaven.

Notice that there was no waiting. There was not a moment of hesitation. Lazarus met Abraham of whom the Bible says, *"It was not through law that Abraham and his offspring received the promise that he would be heir of the world, but through the righteousness that comes by faith" (Romans 4:13),* and, *"Abraham believed God, and it was credited to him as righteousness" (Romans 4:3).* Abraham experienced the same salvation that poor Lazarus did. By the grace of God, both of them were in heaven.

This is not an isolated teaching of the Bible. Jesus reinforced the fact that believers go to heaven right away when He spoke to the thief on the cross. What was going to happen when the newly believing thief died? Jesus said to the repentant criminal, *"Today you will be with me in paradise" (Luke 23:43).* The man would go to heaven right away.

There is no waiting, no limbo, no purgatory, no "pending a final destiny" holding area, and no mysterious dreamlike state for those we love who have died. This clear and comforting truth of the Bible lets us know that if our loved ones knew Christ as their Savior, the angels carried them to the great banquet feast of heaven—just like Lazarus. Right now they are there.

I remember sitting at the bedside of a woman who was near death. Moments before she died she opened her eyes wide, began to smile, and appeared to be looking at a wonderful sight that no one else in the room could see. This believing woman, no doubt, saw the angels coming to carry her to heaven. She wasn't facing a soul sleep or a waiting room. She was heaven-bound! She was experiencing a joyful and immediate face-to-face meeting with Jesus. There was no delay.

Of course, the same immediacy is true for the unbeliever. There's no waiting in that situation either. As you saw in the verses above, the rich man died and was buried. What happened next? Where was he? Jesus said, *"In hell, where he was in torment..."* Later in this book we'll take a closer look at the Bible's teaching about hell. For now, the point is clear: life in heaven or hell begins immediately after death.

Where is heaven? Where is the "paradise" Jesus spoke of to the thief on the cross? And where is hell? Is heaven "up there" and hell "down there"?

After Jesus ascended into heaven, an angel said to the disciples as they looked up into the sky, *"Men of Galilee, why do you stand here looking into the sky? This same Jesus, who has been taken from you into heaven, will come back in the same way you have seen him go into heaven" (Acts 1:11).* Heaven has an "up" orientation in the Bible. In Revelation chapter 21, the New Jerusalem comes down out of heaven (vs.2). Once again, heaven is "up there." In 1 Thessalonians 4:16-17 we hear that Jesus will come down from heaven and gather all believers together in the midst of the clouds. Heaven is described as a place "up there."

Hell, on the other hand, is described as a place "down there." In Revelation 12:9-10 we hear three times that Satan was thrown down. Hell is described as the abyss. It's pictured as a pit in a downward direction.

The Bible also lets us know that heaven and hell are real places. They are tangible locations. Jesus promised His disciples that He would go and prepare a place for them (John 14:2). So, where are these places? We don't know. We use the language of the Bible to describe their locations, but on this side of eternity we don't have the ability to connect with these places. We can speculate about what the eternal and invisible dimension looks like and where it is, but we must wait for God to reveal the details. For now, we know that heaven and hell exist; they are real places; and, one day, we'll find out where they are.

Chapter Two Questions for Thought and Discussion

1. What theories have you heard regarding where a person goes immediately after he or she dies?

2. Why do you think this issue is important to people who lose loved ones?

3. Read 2 Kings 2:1-11 and Matthew 17:1-3. What do these verses tell you about where people go when their lives on this earth end?

4. In your opinion, what has contributed to the confusion over this question?

5. Read John 14:1-3. What do you learn about God's character and attitude through this promise of Jesus?

6. How does the Biblical teaching that you go to heaven or hell immediately after death affect your life now?

7. In what ways can you utilize this teaching to bring comfort or warning to people in your life?

Verse of Assurance: Revelation 21:4 *"[God] will wipe every tear from their eyes. There will be no more death or mourning or crying or pain, for the old order of things has passed away."*

Note how heaven has brought relief to your loved ones:

Who Are You In Heaven?

"The angels carried him to Abraham's side."

Three
Who Are You In Heaven?

+

A distraught husband wondered if he and his wife would recognize each other when he joined her in heaven. His questions were filled with heartache and panic:

"Will she know me?"

"Will I know her?"

"Will she look so different that I'll never find her?"

Jesus said that the angels carried Lazarus to *Abraham's* side. Why did Jesus say that? Why didn't He say, "The angels carried Lazarus to heaven" or "The angels carried Lazarus to paradise" or "The angels carried Lazarus to God"?

Notice that by mentioning Abraham, Jesus was making reference to a real person. Every person listening knew about Abraham. He was the identifiable father of God's people. He was someone every Jewish individual would be thrilled to meet and see. And there he was. Abraham! Alive, talking, and recognizable. Jesus could have left Abraham out of this parable. By including him, however, Jesus gave His listeners the clear and encouraging news that people in heaven are real, can be recognized, and are in wonderful relationship with each other.

The main characters of the parable also reinforced this truth. From hell, the rich man (who was also real, recognizable, and completely himself), *"looked up and saw Abraham far away, with Lazarus by his side" (vs.23b).* The rich man could see and recognize Abraham and Lazarus. Lazarus is the only named character in all of Jesus' parables. I wonder if, by naming this desperate beggar, Jesus was striving to make heaven more real than we tend to make it. I wonder if Jesus also wanted His listeners to comprehend fully how important it is to know the way to heaven--the stakes are real and high. I wonder if, by using the name of one of His good friends (See John 11; Jesus stayed with Mary, Martha, and their brother Lazarus more than once), Jesus created such a personal connection that people couldn't miss the fact that heaven is real and the people there are also real, recognizable and every bit themselves.

That's the way it will be. In heaven you are yourself. In heaven you will recognize people. When people go to heaven, they are immediately themselves. There is no temporary spirit hanging around. There is no mysterious, unknown self. You will be you!

The Bible does make clear, however, that you will not be the old you. Revelation chapter 7 shows the saints in heaven fully restored:

> *Then one of the elders asked me, "These in white robes-- who are they, and where did they come from?" I answered, "Sir, you know." And he said, "These are they who have come out of the great tribulation; they have washed their robes and made them white in the blood of the Lamb. Therefore, they are before the throne of God and serve him day and night in his temple; and he who sits on the throne will spread his tent over them. Never again will they hunger; never again will they thirst. The*

sun will not beat upon them, nor any scorching heat. For the Lamb at the center of the throne will be their shepherd; he will lead them to springs of living water. And God will wipe away every tear from their eyes" (vss. 13-17).

These are forgiven, restored, renewed, and cared for people. There is no pain or want or sadness. These saints are fueled by new hearts and spirits in the presence of God.

In 1 Corinthians chapter 15 Paul described the new self you will have at the final physical resurrection of the body. Our bodies will be different in heaven. He says:

The body that is sown is perishable, it is raised imperishable; it is sown in dishonor, it is raised in glory; it is sown in weakness, it is raised in power; it is sown a natural body, it is raised a spiritual body. If there is a natural body, there is also a spiritual body (vss. 42b-44).

This is very good news. Heaven brings healing and restoration. Sorrow and pain come to an end. But you are still yourself. This applies to the souls of loved ones who wait in heaven for the resurrection of the body, and to all believers who wait on earth for the last day that will come *"in a flash, in the twinkling of an eye, at the last trumpet" (1 Corinthians 15:52).* Remember what happened on the mount of transfiguration. Jesus prayed with Peter, James and John. As He prayed,

The appearance of his face changed, and his clothes became as bright as a flash of lightning. Two men, Moses and Elijah, appeared in glorious splendor, talking with Jesus (vss. 29-31a).

Where were Moses and Elijah living at that time? In heaven! But as they appeared with Jesus, they were very recognizable people. Peter, James, and John—fellow believers who never even met them—recognized them right away. Even in their glorious splendor, Moses and Elijah were themselves and were recognized as themselves.

People are still themselves in heaven. They aren't angels or ghosts or any other kind of spiritual creatures people might dream up. They are themselves. Just as the rich man recognized Abraham and Lazarus and just as Peter, James and John recognized Moses and Elijah, you will recognize your loved ones in heaven. You will also be recognized by them. In heaven you will be yourself. When the day of the resurrection comes, you will have a restored and new resurrection body, but you will be yourself. God created each one of us, and He treasures who we are—even into eternity.

Chapter Three Questions for Thought and Discussion

1. Read Isaiah 43:1. What does this verse tell you about God's investment in and knowledge of your life?

2. If God created your identity, calling you by name, what does this mean for your eternal identity in heaven?

3. How do Jesus' words to the repentant thief on the cross in Luke 23:43 communicate how much God treasures your personal identity?

4. How do you think Peter, James, and John recognized Elijah and Moses?

5. What does this mean for the way you will interact with people in heaven?

6. Talk about who you look forward to meeting most in heaven and why.

7. How are you encouraged by being you, but being a new and restored you, in heaven?

Verse of God's Love: Psalm 139:13 *"For you created my inmost being; you knit me together in my mother's womb."*

Note some personality traits of departed loved ones you look forward to experiencing again in heaven:

Angels

"The angels carried him…"

Four
Angels

+

If you have ever wondered about the existence of angels, Jesus' parable of the rich man and Lazarus shows that these mighty and faithful servants are real and active. When Lazarus died, the angels were ready to carry poor Lazarus to the place prepared for Him by the Savior. Imagine Lazarus' surprise as he received a heavenly escort to his celestial home. No longer was he overlooked as a lowly good-for-nothing. No longer did eyes dart away from his sore-riddled body. Instead, the heavenly gaze of angelic eyes looked deeply into his soul and connected with him on a level he had not experienced in a very long time. Yes, angels were real. They were real and wonderful.

A friend of mine discovered this beautiful fact in a vivid way. He was riding in an old pick-up truck. His friend was driving. They were on a summer landscaping expedition--students making a little money over summer vacation. The driver was wearing his seat belt, but the old truck didn't have a functioning seat belt on the passenger side, so my friend went without one. As they drove at a good clip down a county road, the driver didn't see a car that was pulling out to make a left turn. The crash couldn't be avoided. My friend saw it coming and tried to brace himself. But the impact was too strong. When the truck hit the car, my friend was thrown forward. He saw the windshield and the old metal window frame of the truck getting closer to his head and face. All of a sudden he felt himself being pushed powerfully back into his seat. He bounced against the seatback. After impact, the driver of the truck turned to him with surprise. The driver saw my friend heading toward certain injury. What happened? My friend still felt the soreness on his shoulders where he had been pushed back into his seat. My friend believes that angelic intervention prevented his serious injury in that collision.

But why talk about angels? Is this a sensationalized conversation driven by mystical personal experiences? No. We talk about angels because God talks about them first! God brings up the subject of angels in the Bible. He lets us know that His angelic support staff is real and working in our lives. That's the way the Lord is: for our benefit and confidence, for extra blessing and joy, for a greater awareness of His work in our lives, God reveals the remarkable work of angels.

In Ephesians 6:10-12 St. Paul speaks about the very real, but unseen, spiritual dimension: *"Finally, be strong in the Lord and in his mighty power. Put on the full armor of God so that you can take your stand against the devil's schemes. For our struggle is not against flesh and blood, but against rulers, against the authorities, against the powers of this dark world and against the spiritual forces of evil in the heavenly realms."*

What spiritual forces are out there? The Bible provides some clear answers.

One frequent angelic reference in the Old Testament is the "Angel of the Lord." This is no ordinary angel. In Genesis 16 the Angel of the Lord heard Hagar's request for a child and granted that prayer request. In verse thirteen Hagar equated the Angel of the Lord to God. In Genesis 22:11 the Angel of the Lord stopped Abraham from killing his son Isaac. The angel's closing words of blessing displayed His Godly identity (vss.15-18). Judges 2:1 also reveals the identity of the Angel of the Lord: *"The angel of the Lord went up from Gigal to Bokim and said, 'I brought you up out of Egypt and led you into the land that I swore to give to your forefathers. I said, "I will never break my covenant with you."""* The "Angel of the Lord" refers to the personal assistance of God to His people. The title refers to the tangible appearance of the Savior. Typically, we know this person as Jesus. While He was not yet named in the Old Testament, this intervening and helping presence is recognized as the second person of the Holy Trinity, the Son of God. The title "Angel of the Lord" is a reference to more than an angel. It is a reference to Jesus.

The Bible does contain frequent references to "regular" angels. The Greek word is "angelos." The Hebrew word is "Maleack." Both words mean "messenger." Angels are facts of life in the Bible. These spiritual beings are active and evident. Their reality is beyond debate. Both good angels and evil angels make their way through the pages of Scripture and through the events of our lives. Take a look at some examples of God's good messengers in action:

Genesis 28:12 - *"[Jacob] had a dream in which he saw a stairway resting on the earth with its top reaching to heaven, and the angels of God were ascending and descending on it."*

Job 1:6 - *"One day the angels came to present themselves before the Lord."*

Job 38:6-7 - (regarding creation) *The Lord said, "On what were [the earth's] footings set, or who laid its cornerstone--while the morning stars sang together and the angels shouted for joy?"*

Daniel 6:21-22 - (after the lions' den episode, we hear that angels are powerful and spiritual beings) *"Daniel answered, 'O king, live forever! My God sent his angel, and he shut the mouths of the lions.'"*

Daniel 7:10 (regarding the number of angels surrounding God) - *"Thousands upon thousands attended him; ten thousand times ten thousand stood before him."*

Matthew 18:10 - (Jesus mentions that there are guardian angels serving His people) *Jesus said, "See that you do not look down on one of these little ones. For I tell you that their angels in heaven always see the face of my Father in heaven."*

Hebrews 1:14 - *"Are not all angels ministering spirits sent to serve those who will inherit eternal salvation?"*

Hebrews 12:22-23 - *"But you have come to Mount Zion, to the heavenly Jerusalem, the city of the living God. You have come to thousands upon thousands of angels in joyful assembly, to the church of the firstborn, whose names are written in heaven."*

Hebrews 13:2 - *"Do not forget to entertain strangers, for by so doing some people have entertained angels without knowing it."*

Unfortunately, evil angels also exist. They are aligned with the devil's desire to assert himself against God and to destroy believers. The Bible mentions these evil angels primarily in the context of their destruction. These opposing spiritual forces will not win. The Bible says:

Matthew 25:41 - *[Jesus said] "Then he will say to those on his left, 'Depart from me, you who are cursed, into the eternal fire prepared for the devil and his angels.'"*

2 Peter 2:4 - *"For...God did not spare angels when they sinned, but sent them to hell, putting them into gloomy dungeons to be held for judgment..."*

Revelation 12:9 - "The great dragon was hurled down--that ancient serpent called the devil, or Satan, who leads the whole world astray. He was hurled to the earth, and his angels with him."

Plunging into this spiritual realm is exciting. It stimulates curiosity and opens our eyes to new realities. God wants us to know about His servants who help us. He wants us to be aware of the battle raging behind the scenes. He wants us to be on guard against the thronging forces of evil. But He doesn't want us to get distracted. The most important point about the reality of angels is that they point to the Savior, Jesus. Angels are not an end in themselves. They are servants and messengers. They are not meant to be worshipped or prayed to. The revelation of their existence is not meant to give them precedence over their Creator and Master. The Bible warns about getting angels out of perspective:

Colossians 2:18 - "Do not let anyone who delights in false humility and the worship of angels disqualify you from the prize. Such a person goes into great detail about what he has seen, and his unspiritual mind puffs him up with idle notions."

Revelation 19:10 - (an angel speaks when John fell at his feet to worship him) *"Do not do it! I am a fellow servant with you and with your brothers who hold to the testimony of Jesus. Worship God! For the testimony of Jesus is the spirit of prophecy."*

A discussion about angels always begins and ends with Jesus. During your hustling, bustling, stress-filled life, and as you make your way through times of weakness, fear, loneliness and sadness, the Bible gives you the encouraging word that Jesus is truly with you and that His servants, His angels, surround you.

They are real. They reinforce the real and caring Lord Jesus who is your advocate and friend, your helper and strength.

That is exactly what the Bible has been telling people day after day for thousands of years. In our sin, in our brokenness, we can't go it alone. But *"God so loved the world that he gave his one and only Son, that whoever believes in him shall not perish but have eternal life" (John 3:16).* God intervened with help, hope, and the forgiveness of sins, through Jesus Christ. Angels are part of that intervening help. Angels are God's special support team always at work for His people.

The Biblical examples of angel service are plentiful:

Genesis 3:24 - "After [the Lord God] drove the man out, he placed on the east side of the Garden of Eden cherubim and a flaming sword flashing back and forth to guard the way to the tree of life."

(Note: "Cherubim" is the plural of "Cherub," a special servant of God, understood as a type of angel. Exodus 25:20 describes the cherubim carved on the Ark of the Covenant. The description includes wings. Because of this and the description of seraphim in the Bible (Isaiah 6:2), angels have been portrayed as having wings.)

Genesis 19:1-22 gives the account of the angels that delivered Lot and his family from the corrupt towns of Sodom and Gomorrah. It was personal and miraculous intervention.

Psalm 91:9-12 - "If you make the Most High your dwelling--even the Lord, who is my refuge--then no harm will befall you, no disaster will come near your tent. For he will command his angels concerning you to guard you in all your ways; they will lift you up in their hands, so that you will not strike your foot against a stone."

Psalm 103:20-22 - *"Praise the Lord, you his angels, you mighty ones who do his bidding, who obey his word. Praise the Lord, all his heavenly hosts, you his servants who do his will. Praise the Lord, all his works everywhere in his dominion."*

Matthew 1:18-21 - *"This is how the birth of Jesus Christ came about: His mother Mary was pledged to be married to Joseph, but before they came together, she was found to be with child through the Holy Spirit. Because Joseph her husband was a righteous man and did not want to expose her to public disgrace, he had in mind to divorce her quietly. But after he had considered this, an angel of the Lord appeared to him in a dream and said, 'Joseph son of David, do not be afraid to take Mary home as your wife, because what is conceived in her is from the Holy Spirit. She will give birth to a son, and you are to give him the name Jesus, because he will save his people from their sins.'"*

Matthew 13:39 - *"The harvest is the end of the age, and the harvesters are angels."*

Matthew 13:49 - *"This is how it will be at the end of the age. The angels will come and separate the wicked from the righteous."*

Matthew 25:31 - *"When the Son of Man comes in his glory, and all the angels with him..."*

Matthew 28:2-3 - *"There was a violent earthquake, for an angel of the Lord came down from heaven and, going to the tomb, rolled back the stone and sat on it. His appearance was like lightning, and his clothes were white as snow."*

Mark 1:13 - *"And [Jesus] was in the desert forty days, being tempted by Satan. He was with the wild animals, and angels attended him."*

Luke 22:43 - "An angel from heaven appeared to [Jesus in the garden of Gethsemane] and strengthened him."

Acts 8:26 - "Now an angel of the Lord said to Philip, 'Go south to the road--the desert road--that goes down from Jerusalem to Gaza.'"

Acts 12:6-11 - "The night before Herod was to bring him to trial, Peter was sleeping between two soldiers, bound with two chains, and sentries stood guard at the entrance. Suddenly an angel of the Lord appeared and a light shone in the cell. He struck Peter on the side and woke him up. 'Quick, get up!' he said, and the chains fell off Peter's wrists. Then the angel said to him, 'Put on your clothes and sandals.' And Peter did so. 'Wrap your cloak around you and follow me,' the angel told him. Peter followed him out of the prison, but he had no idea that what the angel was doing was really happening; he thought he was seeing a vision. They passed the first and second guards and came to the iron gate leading to the city. It opened for them by itself, and they went through it. When they had walked the length of one street, suddenly the angel left him. Then Peter came to himself and said, 'Now I know without a doubt that the Lord sent his angel and rescued me from Herod's clutches and from everything the Jewish people were anticipating.'"

Acts 12:23 - "Immediately, because Herod did not give praise to God, an angel of the Lord struck him down, and he was eaten by worms and died."

1 Thessalonians 4:16 - "For the Lord himself will come down from heaven, with a loud command, with the voice of the archangel and with the trumpet call of God, and the dead in Christ will rise first."

The Bible also describes some "personality traits" and characteristics of angels. We know two names of angels: Michael and Gabriel. Michael is described as a leader and an archangel (Daniel 10:13, 21; 12:1; Jude 9; Revelation 12:7). Gabriel appeared in the book of Daniel (8:16 and 9:21), identified himself to Zechariah, and was mentioned as he appeared to Mary, the mother of Jesus (Luke 1:19, 26). In addition to these two names, the Bible gives even greater detail about what angels are like and what part they play in God's creation:

Luke 15:10 - "There is rejoicing in the presence of the angels of God over one sinner who repents."

Luke 20:34-36 - "Jesus replied, 'The people of this age marry and are given in marriage. But those who are considered worthy of taking part in that age and in the resurrection from the dead will neither marry nor be given in marriage, and they can no longer die; for they are like the angels.'"

1 Corinthians 6:3 - "Do you not know that we will judge angels?"

Hebrews 1:4 - "So [Jesus] became as much superior to the angels as the name he has inherited is superior to theirs."

1 Peter 1:12 mentions *"the things that have now been told you by those who have preached the gospel to you by the Holy Spirit sent from heaven."* Then Peter adds, *"Even angels long to look into these things."* The special servants of God see the wonder of the life of Jesus given for us.

Angels are unique and interesting. We can't understand everything about them, but we rejoice that with the saving work of God comes the crowd of His heavenly servants to help us. They may help to protect you or guide you. They may defend you from danger or enemies. They may nudge you in the side to wake you up. They may keep you out of trouble. They may carry you to heaven.   Angels do God's will, answer His call, and serve His people.

They also brought the most important message in history. They heralded the news of Jesus' birth and helped navigate the Messiah's journey on this earth. Picture in your mind these familiar and wonderful angel episodes from the Bible:

Matthew 1:20-21 - "But after [Joseph] had considered [divorcing Mary], an angel of the Lord appeared to him in a dream and said, 'Joseph son of David, do not be afraid to take Mary home as your wife, because what is conceived in her is from the Holy Spirit. She will give birth to a son, and you are to give him the name Jesus, because he will save his people from their sins.'"

Matthew 2:13 - "But after [the wise men] had gone, an angel of the Lord appeared to Joseph in a dream. 'Get up,' he said, 'take the child and his mother and escape into Egypt. Stay there until I tell you, for Herod is going to search for the child to kill him.'" After Herod died an angel appeared in a dream again to Joseph to let him know it was safe to return (Matthew 2:19-20).

Luke 1:26-38 - "In the sixth month, God sent the angel Gabriel to Nazareth, a town in Galilee, to a virgin pledged to be married to a man named Joseph, a descendant of David. The virgin's name was Mary. The angel went to her and said, 'Greetings, you who are highly favored! The Lord is with you.' Mary was greatly troubled at his words and wondered what kind of greeting this might be. But the angel said to her, 'Do not be afraid, Mary, you have found favor with God. You will be with child and give birth to a son, and you are to give him the name Jesus. He will be great and will be called Son of the Most High. The Lord God will give him the throne of his father David, and he will reign over the house of Jacob forever; his kingdom will never end.' 'How will this be,'

Mary asked the angel, 'since I am a virgin?' The angel answered, 'The Holy Spirit will come upon you, and the power of the most high God will overshadow you. So the holy one to be born will be called the Son of God. Even Elizabeth your relative is going to have a child in her old age, and she who was said to be barren is in her sixth month. For nothing is impossible with God.' 'I am the Lord's servant,' Mary answered. 'May it be to me as you have said.' Then the angel left her."

Luke 2:8-15 - "And there were shepherds living out in the fields nearby, keeping watch over their flocks at night. An angel of the Lord appeared to them, and the glory of the Lord shone around them, and they were terrified. But the angel said to them, 'Do not be afraid. I bring you good news of great joy that will be for all people. Today in the town of David a Savior has been born to you; he is Christ the Lord. This will be a sign to you: you will find a baby wrapped in cloths and lying in a manger.' Suddenly a great company of heavenly host appeared with the angel, praising God and saying, 'Glory to God in the highest, and on earth peace, good will among men.' When the angels had left them and gone into heaven, the shepherds said to one another, 'Let's go to Bethlehem and see this thing that has happened, which the Lord has told us about.'"

The angels packed the countryside. They stepped into homes. They surprised people they visited. But their point was not to draw attention to themselves. It was to point to the Savior Jesus!

This chapter about angels is not meant to confuse or to cause us to adore angels. It is not meant to take attention away from Jesus. On the contrary, it is to point to Him. It is to point to God's commitment to serving you and caring for you in a broken world, during a busy life, through a barrage of information, and wherever you go. Angels point to the Savior, to the One born in Bethlehem, to the one who gave His life on the cross for you, to the one who rose on Easter morning. Angels rejoice in the forgiveness of sins and eternal life for God's people. Angels are thrilled with the worship and adoration of their Lord God. The focus is always on Jesus. Our God of grace sends His angels to help us focus and to fight for us. The armies of God are in your life and are contending for you as you wait for Jesus to come again and as you wait for them to usher you to heaven.

What if you never have an angel encounter? That's impossible! You may never know it or see it, but God's promise is that His angels are always watching over you and serving you. And as long as you are looking to Jesus--your Savior who gave His life for you, forgives you, and loves you, the angels are rejoicing! As long as you are hearing God's Word and living the new life the Lord gives, you're walking with His angels. That's the best encounter of all. The glory isn't in the flash of an angel meeting. The glory and the story are Jesus Christ!

Chapter Four Questions for Thought and Discussion

1. Read Daniel 3:1-28.   How have you seen God's protection at key moments in your life?

2. Who was in the fire with the three men?

3. What does this episode tell you about God's commitment to your life?

4. Look through the verses on pages 35-36. Choose two or three verses that impact you most. Explain what they mean to you.

5. Read Genesis 19:1-22. How did the angels serve God's people and what does their service mean for your life today?

6. Pages 40-41 describe some of the "personality traits" of angels. Think about and discuss what information and insight these verses provide.

7. Talk about any new understanding and new questions you have about angels after reading this chapter.

Verse of God's Confidence: Psalm 91:11 *"For he will command his angels concerning you to guard you in all your ways."*

Note some ways that God has brought you confidence and help during your times of grief:

Is There a Connection Between the Living and the Dead?

"Send Lazarus to my father's house…"

Five
Is There a Connection Between the Living and the Dead?

+

"I still talk to her."

John was referring to his wife. She was only 34 when she died. They had two young daughters. Now John was alone, but for some reason he felt that he wasn't completely alone.

"Do you think we're still connected in some way?" he asked.

I'll never forget another dear lady, Lydia, as she described the mysterious sense of closeness she experienced with her son-in-law after he died. Then there was Roger, a man who lost his wife after nearly fifty years of marriage. He told me about a moment in his kitchen when he sensed his wife was right there.

What were these people experiencing? Was it possible that a connection still existed with their loved ones? Or did death create a divide that was too vast for any connection to exist anymore?

Loved ones on earth wonder if death destroys the relational connection they treasured and cultivated this side of heaven. Was the relationship insignificant? Was it an inconsequential blip on the radar of eternity? Or do our relationships on this side of heaven have a lasting meaning? Is there a deeper significance and connection with spouses, children, and close friends? Is there something eternal that knits us together and keeps us together?

Some philosophies and religions say that death ends everything. They assert that once life is over there is nothing left. But God points us in a different direction. Indications in the Bible lead us to see a deep, meaningful, and eternal significance in our earthly relationships. In our world broken by sin, our relationships are but a shadow of what they are meant to be. But this life is not all there is. And the relationships established so carefully and lovingly by God are the beginning of something far greater and more enduring.

John, Roger, Lydia, and others forced me to think hard about what we confess in the Apostle's Creed: "I believe in the communion of saints." Could this teaching help answer the question about a connection between those who have gone to be with the Lord and believers who are still waiting to join Him? Might this Biblical doctrine help us answer whether death creates a total separation from ones we care about or if a bond still exists to our loved ones who died in faith?

Revelation chapter 7 paints a picture of heaven's throne room. All those who have *"come out of the great tribulation"* and *"have washed their robes and made them white in the blood of the Lamb"* are *"before the throne of God and serve him day and night in his temple" (vss.14-15).* John goes on to say that they are gathered around the Lamb who is at the center of the throne (vs.17).

In addition to that Biblical description of the saints in heaven, Jesus said to His living disciples in Matthew 28:20, *"I am with you always, to the very end of the age."*

What do those two realities add up to? They add up to the teaching called "The Communion of Saints." The phrase is an expression that describes the Church, the gathering of God's redeemed people. Part of the teaching means that all who have died in Christ and all who live in Christ are connected as a community in Christ. All believers on earth and in heaven share an amazing and encouraging oneness through Jesus Christ. He is the connector. The One who gives life is the eternal link between heaven and earth. Through His death and resurrection, Jesus made sure that death did not create an eternal divide. Death did not have the last word. Jesus' redeemed people who died are alive forever with Him.

That is good news for every believer. Here on earth no believer is alone. A living and active community of people made holy by the blood of Jesus is alive and well. This group of people, called the Church, fills heaven and the earth. As the saints who have gone before us actively celebrate Jesus' victory over sin and death, they also rally around us and stand with us as we walk by faith this side of heaven. The believers in heaven are "the great cloud of witnesses" mentioned in Hebrews 12:1. They are the saints who cheer us on in the race that has been marked out for us.

In other words, Jesus keeps us together! In Him, a connection still exists.

God wants to comfort us with this great news. The Bible teaches with all certainty that we are not far from our loved ones who have died in faith. The closer we are to Jesus, the closer our loved ones are to us. The distance is minimal. The separation is miniscule.

This good news frees us from some pitfalls. First, we can be certain that our relationships are precious to God. The time, energy, and sacrifice we invest do not go to waste. In fact, our relationships here on earth are just a small taste of the full and complete relationships we will experience in eternity. When Jesus commented in Luke 20 that there is no marriage in heaven, He wasn't diminishing the value of the marriage relationship on earth. He wasn't telling us that husbands and wives will be cast away into an anonymous eternity, never to be in relationship again. Jesus was emphasizing that eternity is different. It transcends the limitations of our broken earthly existence. Heaven will be much better. The resurrection will exceed our expectations. Relationships will be so full and wonderful, we'll wonder why we even tried to compare our fragile and imperfect earthly connections to the beauty and fullness God has in store for us. Relationships matter to God. Your love for precious people in your life will be more complete than ever in heaven.

Second, we do not have to seek after mysterious experiences in order to reconnect with loved ones beyond the grave. How may people have ventured into distracting and dangerous spiritual practices to hear from a loved one who has died? As we are knit together in Christ, we have confidence that our connection to and closeness with fellow believers who have died is strong and living. The way to get closer to loved ones who have died is to draw closer to Jesus, not to seek our own ways or earthly gimmicks. Even Abraham, in Luke 16, told the rich man that his brothers would be better off paying attention to God's Word rather than seeing a dead person come back to life. In our grief and pain, the Bible always directs us to Jesus. He is the One who keeps us connected.

Finally, the good news of the communion of saints frees us from despair. Jesus said, *"I am coming soon" (Rev. 22:12).* With Him will come our loved ones who have died in faith. We have much to look forward to. We have hope. A reunion awaits us. A good life, a complete life, created and prepared by our Savior, is very close. There is reason to keep going, to keep living. The Apostle Paul encouraged believers with the news of the resurrection in 1 Corinthians chapter 15. As believers on earth heard about the glory of heaven, they may have wished they could be there immediately. We feel the same way at times, especially if someone precious is there waiting for us. In verse fifty-eight, Paul answers this yearning by telling us that God still has a purpose and plan for us here on earth. His work is important. Paul declared, *"Therefore, my dear brothers, stand firm. Let nothing move you. Always give yourselves fully to the work of the Lord, because you know that your labor in the Lord is not in vain."*

As we work and wait, however, we can rejoice. In Jesus, we are close to and connected with fellow believers on earth and in heaven. Your thoughts about loved ones, your conversations with them out loud or in your head, your heart that yearns for them in the middle of the night when it is so difficult to sleep, are not wasteful actions or meaningless fantasies. They are the acts of people who know that their Redeemer lives, that their redeemed loved ones live with Him, and that one day you will see each other again.

1. Read Revelation 7:9-17. In verse fourteen, an elder identifies this group of people. Who are they and what are they doing?

2. How do these verses encourage you as you think about loved ones who have died?

3. Read Hebrews 12:1-3. Hebrews chapter 11 reviewed the "faith hall of fame," people who trusted God and gave their lives confessing His name. What is their role in our walk of faith according to Hebrews 12?

4. How do these verses direct your focus as you navigate the struggles of life--especially as you miss loved ones?

5. This chapter discussed the teaching of the "communion of saints." How does this teaching impact your outlook as you make your way through life on earth?

6. Read Matthew 17:1-5. How does this account of Jesus' transfiguration reinforce the teaching of the communion of saints?

7. How are you sometimes like Peter? What did God's statement teach Peter, and what does it teach you about what your focus needs to be as you think about ones who have died?

Verse of God's Presence: Deuteronomy 31:6 *"The LORD your God goes with you; he will never leave you nor forsake you."*

Note some ways that you've notice God's presence in your life:

The Resurrection and Judgment Day

"Let him warn them, so that they will not also come to this place of torment."

Six
The Resurrection and Judgment Day

+

Some of the most hope-giving words ever spoken by Jesus were His words from the cross to a repentant thief. The brief conversation is recorded in Luke 23:42-43. The thief said to the Savior, *"Jesus, remember me when you come into your kingdom."* Jesus replied, *"I tell you the truth, today you will be with me in paradise."*

That very day, the forgiven thief would be joining Jesus in heaven. There would be no waiting, no delay, no soul-sleep, no biding time until the end of the age came around. As we saw in the previous chapter, the forgiven man would join the cloud of witnesses in heaven. There would be no more pain and no more tears. He would serve God in an exciting and fulfilling eternal kingdom.

But the Bible also says, *"Listen, I tell you a mystery: We will not all sleep, but we will all be changed--in a flash, in the twinkling of an eye, at the last trumpet. For the trumpet will sound, the dead will be raised imperishable, and we will be changed"* (1 Corinthians 15:51-52).

On one hand, the Bible says that we wait for the last day to be raised. On the other hand, Jesus said that the thief would be in heaven right away.

One of the most commonly misunderstood teachings of the Bible is how eternal life and the final judgment work together. Jesus said that Lazarus went to Abraham's side.

Lazarus was in heaven. But what about Paul's comment in 1 Thessalonians 4?

> *Brothers, we do not want you to be ignorant about those who fall asleep, or to grieve like the rest of men, who have no hope. We believe that Jesus died and rose again and so we believe that God will bring with Jesus those who have fallen asleep in him. According to the Lord's own word, we tell you that we who are still alive, who are left till the coming of the Lord, will certainly not precede those who have fallen asleep. For the Lord himself will come down from heaven, with a loud command, with the voice of the archangel and with the trumpet call of God, and the dead in Christ will rise first. After that, we who are still alive and are left will be caught up together with them in the clouds to meet the Lord in the air. And so we will be with the Lord forever. Therefore encourage each other with these words (vss.13-18).*

And how do Jesus' words from Matthew 25 fit in?

> *When the Son of Man comes in his glory, and all the angels with him, he will sit on his throne in heavenly glory. All the nations will be gathered before him, and he will separate the people one from another as a shepherd separates the sheep from the goats. He will put the sheep on his right and the goats on his left...Then they will go away to eternal punishment, but the righteous to eternal life (vss. 31-33, 46).*

Hebrews 9:27 makes it clear that *"man is destined to die once, and after that to face judgment."* So, when is the judgment and how do all these statements fit with Jesus' own words about the immediacy of heaven or hell for those who die?

Do these Biblical statements create a conflict in the Scriptures? How can we reconcile these two ideas? What is the Bible telling us?

Let's talk about what we know. Lazarus died and went to heaven. The rich man died and went to hell. They were judged. Their eternal lives were being lived. They truly did die once and face judgment.

What was Paul talking about in 1 Corinthians and in 1 Thessalonians? Notice that he was speaking to believers who were still alive. The people in Corinth were concerned about the reality of the resurrection. Paul let them know with certainty that the resurrection would happen. They would be brand new.

The people in Thessalonica were worried about their loved ones who died. Paul was assuring these living believers that their loved ones did not disappear and that they would not be forgotten. In fact, Paul said that they would "rise first." Did that mean that these faith-filled loved ones were waiting in limbo, separated from Jesus, and disconnected with fellow saints? No. The Greek verb for "rise" in 1 Thessalonians 4:16 paints the picture of "rising up," standing up," "coming," and "appearing." Paul was letting these worried living believers know that they would see their loved ones again when Jesus appeared. These departed loved ones would be made visible to those living on earth in the great resurrection of the body on the last day. All people would finally see what has been true all along. The redeemed people of God were alive with Christ. They were being taken care of. And on the great Day of Judgment, believers who were still alive would join them "in the air" with

Christ, so that together, all believers would be together in the eternal care of Jesus.

Paul was talking about Judgment Day, the final day, the day all the inhabitants of heaven and earth and hell will come together for the final pronouncement of everyone's eternal destiny. On that day all will see what, before, we could only see as "a poor reflection" in a mirror. On Judgment Day we will see "face to face" (1 Corinthians 13:12).

That was Jesus' message in Matthew 25. In this life, the day and hour is unknown (Matthew 24:36). In this world we work for an unseen treasure (Matthew 25:14ff). But the final day is coming when the pronouncement about our faith and the fruits of our faith will be made known to all. The sheep and goats judgment in Matthew 25 is all about making the unseen seen. Everything in life will be weighed on the scales of faith and unfaith. Everyone will see everything clearly. This judgment is the once and for all day of public judgment that will usher in the eternal kingdom.

Was Jesus saying that all who had already died before Judgment Day were in spiritual limbo? Not at all. He was simply making clear that on the day of final judgment everyone will be gathered together, everyone will see each other, the living will be judged, final judgment will be pronounced for the living and the dead, and everyone will see from the eternal Judge's point of view. It will truly be the day of the resurrection of all flesh.

Revelation chapter 7 describes the saints who have come out of the great tribulation. The chapter paints a picture of their active service for Jesus. They surround God's throne and "serve him day and night in his temple" (vs. 15). This is not an inactive, waiting-in-limbo situation. These are active servants of God, the spirits of the redeemed dwelling with Jesus, using their gifts in the way God intended.

Revelation chapter 20 mentions believers who have already died. It says that they experienced the "first resurrection" and reign with Christ:

> *I saw thrones on which were seated those who had been given authority to judge. And I saw the souls of those who had been beheaded because of their testimony for Jesus and because of the word of God. They had not worshiped the beast or his image and had not received his mark on their foreheads or their hands. They came to life and reigned with Christ a thousand years. (The rest of the dead did not come to life until the thousand years were ended.) This is the first resurrection. Blessed and holy are those who have part in the first resurrection. The second death has no power over them, but they will be priests of God and of Christ and will reign with him for a thousand years (vss. 4-6).*

Jesus mentions the resurrection at the last day, the final judgment, in John chapter 6:

> *And this is the will of him who sent me, that I shall lose none of all that he has given me, but raise them up at the last day. For my Father's will is that everyone who looks to the Son and believes in him shall have eternal life, and I will raise him up at the last day (vss. 39-40).*

Clearly, judgment—the eternal determination of heaven or hell, and the commencement of that life, happens immediately at the time of death. Judgment for ones who are still living and the public and universal recognition and pronouncement of the judgment of all people who have already died, happens on the day Jesus raises all people bodily and gathers all people together again—the day we call Judgment Day.

The book of Revelation offers clarity that brings us comfort. There are two deaths: physical death and eternal death. There are also two resurrections: the entry into heaven of those who die before the end of the world and the bodily resurrection of the Lord's redeemed on the Last Day.

Revealing these facts about death and resurrection is not meant to be confusing. In fact, the opposite is true. This side of heaven we wonder about the mystery of death and the afterlife. As we grieve the death of loved ones, we are concerned about their care. Our gracious God fills us in on some key facts. First, those who die in faith are blessed. They live with Jesus in paradise. As Paul said in 1 Thessalonians, this teaching is meant for our comfort.

Second, the day is coming when everyone will appear before the throne of the risen Savior. We are called to be prepared for this great Day of Judgment. God gives us fair warning. Time is limited. For us and for the people we're called to reach, the message of salvation in Jesus is urgent. As Paul said in 1 Corinthians 6:2, *"Now is the time of God's favor, now is the day of salvation."* Any conversation about the resurrection and judgment never stops with our loved ones who have died or with the condition of our own souls. The conversation must spill over into our concern about the many people around us who are not prepared, and into our action for those who do not know the gift of new life in Jesus. Now is the time to urgently and powerfully show and tell the love of Jesus.

Chapter Six Questions for Thought and Discussion

1. Read Matthew 25:1-13. What is the point of this story told by Jesus?

2. What does this parable tell you about how this world will end and what obstacles, temptations, and responsibilities exist as you wait for the end?

3. Read 1 Thessalonians 4:13-15. These three verses contain a great deal of hope. Find as many reasons for hope as you can in the verses and talk about why they encourage you as you think about your loved ones in heaven.

4. Read 1 Thessalonians 4:16-17. In your own words, describe the events captured by these two verses. What might you be thinking and feeling on this amazing day?

5. In view of your thoughts and feelings about the Last Day, what changes or new directions might be needed in your life today?

6. Read Revelation 20:4-6. Who do these verses describe? Talk about their character on earth and God's plan for them in heaven.

7. What are your biggest questions and fears about death and Judgment Day?

Verse of God's Promise: Job 19:25-26 *"I know that my Redeemer lives, and that in the end he will stand upon the earth. And after my skin has been destroyed, yet in my flesh I will see God."*

Note how the reunion in heaven that awaits you gives you encouragement here on earth:

Will Heaven Be Boring?

"Son, remember that in your lifetime you received your good things, while Lazarus received bad things, but now he is comforted here..."

Seven
Will Heaven Be Boring?

+

I've been told with some regularity by both young people and older people that they don't look forward to being in heaven. Why? They don't want to be bored. How exciting can it be, after all, to strum a harp while sitting on a cloud for ETERNITY?

That's the kind of press heaven has received in our culture. Hell has been portrayed as the place where everyone has fun (we'll talk about hell in the next chapter), but heaven has been characterized as a place of sterile nothingness. If you don't like the color white, the texture of clouds, harp music, and singing, heaven looks like a letdown.

But is that portrayal of heaven accurate? Jesus called heaven paradise. The Bible refers to eternity as a new heaven and new earth. The building materials and residents of heaven described in Revelation chapters 21 and 22 make heaven sound pretty upscale--no one-star critic's rating in sight!

So, what is heaven like? Will it be boring, or is there more to the heaven story? What are your loved ones doing in heaven? Are they in line for endless harp lessons and choir recitals? Are they twiddling their thumbs as they wait for Jesus to usher in Judgment Day?

The Bible gives some compelling clues. In Genesis 2:15 we hear that *"God took the man and put him in the Garden of Eden to work it and take care of it."* Verse eighteen says that the man even needed a helper! There was a lot to do. One task mentioned in Genesis was the job of naming the animals (19-20a). What was going on here? The man and woman, who were still living in a perfect world at that time, were working! They were occupied with creative and stimulating tasks. They were enjoying the beauty of creation. They were being challenged to serve by using their gifts. They were finding fulfillment in the jobs God gave them. In paradise, the first man and woman were not bored at all.

Why would our new paradise be any different? Revelation 7:15 says that people in heaven *"are before the throne of God and serve him day and night in his temple."* The word for "serve," is the Greek word "latreuo." This word conveys the sense of service to God, acts of worship. In the New Testament the word is translated as "to worship" or "to serve." It captures the idea that we are called to glorify God in everything we do. Romans 12:1 uses the word when it urges believers to *"offer your bodies as living sacrifices, holy and pleasing to God- -this is your spiritual act of **worship**."* The word is not referring to a church service. It captures the whole-life, God-glorifying service of God's people, praising Him with every spiritual gift and through the vast array of creative and fulfilling tasks God has given us to do.

God's redeemed people serve Him in heaven. Revelation 22:3 emphasizes the point when it declares, *"his servants will serve him."* Heaven is a place of stimulating and creative activity. It is a place where we will find our niche, our calling, and our purpose. It is a place where we will be engaged in what we were created to do. If you've ever jumped out of bed in the morning, eager to tackle the tasks that awaited you, you've experienced a taste of heaven. If you have ever felt the excitement and thrill of doing what you love, seeing the hours pass by like seconds, not wanting the day to end, you've tasted the absolute joy of serving in heaven. Heaven is not boring. It is interesting, fulfilling, satisfying, and energizing. It is the fullness of what we only experience partially and occasionally in our broken world. Your loved ones are not twiddling their thumbs on clouds in heaven. And they're playing harps only if they've craved harp-playing for their entire lives. Your loved ones are using their gifts to serve the One they were created to serve. They are actively engaged in doing the desires of their hearts and living out what they were always meant to do.

But let's talk about those clouds. Heaven's landscape has also been described in a fairly boring way. The colors of heaven I envisioned as I grew up were white, light blue, and gold. I pictured a palette of washed out tones that floated by like puffy clouds on a hazy summer day. It wasn't very appealing. I preferred the earth. I loved the deep red of a nesting cardinal, the vivid green of fresh spring leaves, the shiny black of a late-summer cricket, and the bright yellow of blooming buttercups. Heaven seemed so sterile and dull compared to the vivid beauty of the earth.

But once again, the Bible steers us in a different direction than our dull notions of heaven. Bursting forth from heaven in the book of Revelation are vivid rainbows (4:3, 10:1). Deep and rich blues, purples, greens, and yellows cascade into sight in the descriptions of the gems that adorn the heavenly city (chapter 21). Clear water and newly blooming trees are described as part of the heavenly landscape (chapter 22). The prophet Isaiah brings animals into the picture of heaven. He mentions lions, lambs, oxen, goats, leopards, and calves (11:6, 65:25). Heaven is not a one-dimensional, fuzzy, black and white photo of the "old days." It is the multi-dimensional, clear and breathtaking, full and complete experience of creation as you've never seen it before.

And there's more. Revelation 22:17 says, *"Whoever is thirsty, let him come; and whoever wishes, let him take the free gift of the water of life."* Isaiah 25:6 describes heaven as the mountain of the Lord where he *"will prepare a feast of rich food for all peoples, a banquet of aged wine--the best of meats and the finest of wines."* These descriptions are deeply sensory. This is eating and drinking, thirst-quenching and gustatory delight. These are tastes like you've never tasted before. Heaven is described as a place that touches every sense in a vivid and wonderful way. The experience is rich and full. All of this is not for the purpose of self-indulgence. The overwhelming fullness of experience flows out of God's complete presence and His abundant love. These experiences are what come with the redemption and healing of our sinful and broken lives. Dwelling with God as restored human beings cannot even be captured by words. It's that good. It's that wonderful. It's the total opposite of dull, the antithesis of boring.

But what about eternity? That seems like a very long time. Wouldn't anyone get bored--even with all kinds of great sights, experiences and activities--if they kept going on and on forever? This is where we need to be very clear about the definition of eternity.

What does it mean to live in eternity? Is eternity an ongoing progression of events—like the endless singing and harp playing that some imagine heaven to be? Does eternity mean that everything just goes on and on and on forever? No. That would be a description of *infinity*. Infinity involves an endless progression of events. When you keep counting and never come to an end, that's infinity. The Bible gives the promise of *eternal* life not *infinite* life. Eternity means that there is no time—everything is an endless *now.* It's difficult for us to understand existence without time, with no passing of event after event. But there is no time in heaven. Eternal life means that we live in the moment--a full, stimulating, and exciting moment. Heaven is a constant moment of restoration and wholeness. There is no yesterday or tomorrow. There is no waiting. There is no boredom. There is only the joy of experiencing fulfilling service to God in an eternal moment of the community and beauty of heaven.

What about sleep? It's nice to take a Sunday afternoon nap once in a while. Will we be able to enjoy a snooze now and then in heaven? One thing we know is that there will be no weariness or fatigue. The curse of sin that brings sweat and exhaustion will be gone. But even God rested on the seventh day after His act of creation. Hebrews chapter four calls our life with God a life that enters His rest. Healthy and holy rest may be a part of the blessing of heaven.

If there is no yesterday or tomorrow, do people in heaven remember what they went through on earth? Did Lazarus remember his suffering? Did he have a bad day occasionally when he recalled his lousy stay on earth? Did he remember the rich man and his uncaring behavior? Did he recall friends on earth—just as the rich man thought about his brothers (Luke 16:27-28)? Did he feel guilty or sad about the rich man being in hell?

What do your loved ones remember? Do they remember long and wonderful marriages, relationships with children, blessings and joys that life brought? If they remember the good things, what about the bad? Do they feel the pain and disappointment of the hurt they experienced in life? Do they feel guilt about people who are in hell?

Revelation chapter 7 tells us that there will be no hunger or thirst or suffering in heaven (vs. 16). There will be no tears or sadness (vs. 17; 21:4). Isaiah 25:8 says that the Lord *"will wipe away the tears from all faces; he will remove the disgrace of his people from all the earth."* Clearly, the redeemed in heaven have nothing hurtful in their lives any more. They are healthy, happy, and whole. They experience pure joy.

As we discussed in chapter five, people in heaven are still connected to fellow believers on earth through Jesus. The communion of saints assures us of the value of our relationships and the enduring nature of our oneness in Christ.

But we don't know about memories. Abraham referenced Lazarus' hard times and the rich man's pleasure during their time on earth. Yet, Lazarus carried no burden of sorrow or pain. Abraham communicated with the suffering rich man in hell. It was a sad situation, but we know that neither Abraham nor Lazarus had to bear the heaviness of sadness in their hearts.

How does this work? We don't know. Can loved ones in heaven rejoice in the blessings and celebrations of dear ones on earth? Again, we don't know. We know that there is rejoicing in heaven when a sinner repents (Luke 15:7). But we don't know the details of how the events on earth and the experience of heaven work together. We just know that God, in His mercy, makes it all work very well. We can trust Him that everything is functioning in a way that is much better than we could ever imagine. God is faithful. He is caring for all of His people both in heaven and on earth. We can trust the Lord with the lives of our loved ones and we can trust that He will take care of the details that we can't understand. We know that He has done, and will continue to do, all things well.

We also know that the mystery and glory of heaven is anything but boring. Heaven is an exciting place. Here on earth we yearn to know more about it. We wonder about the fantastic details of paradise. I like to compare what we know about heaven to the Sears Christmas Catalogue. When I was a kid, we eagerly anticipated the arrival of this Christmas wish book. It was filled with pictures and descriptions of the latest toys. My brothers and I fought over who would look through the catalogue first. We scoured the pages to determine what we would put on our Christmas wish list. We were filled with awe as we turned each page and discovered new treasures. But the catalogue was only a shadow, only a fuzzy representation of the real toys. It was printed in black and white. The pictures were small and grainy. We were very excited about the wish book, but the book was nothing compared to the real thing.

I remember putting a battery-operated helicopter from the catalogue on my Christmas list. The helicopter really flew. It was an amazing toy, and I wanted it badly. I dreamed about it. I hurt for it. Then, on Christmas morning that year, I opened a package and there it was! I couldn't believe my eyes. It was red with a yellow propeller. It smelled fresh and new. The battery holder was heavy, but the helicopter was light and agile. It flew powerfully, with the whirring propeller creating a rush of air and a dangerous threat to any heads that got in the way! The helicopter was better and more beautiful than I ever imagined.

In living color, there was no comparison to the description in the catalogue.

The Bible gives us the "catalogue description" of heaven. It is wonderful and exciting, but it is no comparison to the real thing. We will be awed. We will be blown away. We will be thrilled when we see the full-color, up-close-and-personal reality of heaven. Boredom? Not a chance.

Chapter Seven Questions for Thought and Discussion

1. Read Isaiah 25:6-9. God's dwelling place, heaven, is referenced as His mountain: Mount Zion. What impressions of heaven do these verses give?

2. Read Matthew 25:31-36. Note how Jesus refers to the gift of heaven. What image of heaven do His words and phrases depict?

3. Read John 14:1-3. What did Jesus say about the thought and planning put into paradise? What impact will this have on the boredom level of heaven?

4. Read 2 Corinthians 12:1-7. When we read these verses, we usually focus on Paul's thorn in the flesh, but what picture of paradise do these verses give?

5. After reading the sections of Scripture in questions 1-4, discuss the characteristics of heaven and reasons why it is a place to look forward to.

6. Read Revelation chapters 21-22. Make a list of all the reasons why heaven will be exciting, stimulating, and comforting.

7. Think and talk about ways you can communicate the reality of heaven better. What new insights about heaven has this chapter given you?

Verse of God's Affirmation: Matthew 25:21 *"Well done, good and faithful servant! You have been faithful with a few things; I will put you in charge of many things. Come and share your master's happiness."*

Note what you look forward to doing most in heaven:

What About Hell?

"In hell, where he was in torment, he looked up and saw Abraham far away, with Lazarus by his side. So he called to him, 'Father Abraham, have pity on me and send Lazarus to dip the tip of his finger in water and cool my tongue, because I am in agony in this fire.'"

Eight
What About Hell?

+

So far, most of the talk about the afterlife in this book has been dedicated to life in heaven. But what about the alternative? What about the torment of the rich man in hell? There has been a lot of conversation and speculation about hell recently. People are raising some compelling questions: Why would God have hell as an eternal option for our lives? Is it real? Is it fair? Does it mean that God is cruel?

When Jesus told the story of the rich man and Lazarus, He acknowledged that hell was a fact, that it was fair, and that it fit into the eternal plan. But how can we understand the teaching about hell in the Bible? How can we accept the frightening prospect of eternal punishment for anyone?

First, let's make sure we have a good grasp of the subject. The word "hell" occurs fourteen times in the New Testament. The Greek word is "gehenna." You've probably heard that expression before. Jesus is the one who mentions the word in twelve of the fourteen times it is used in the New Testament. The Bible mentions hell in many other ways, too. It is called Hades, eternal punishment, eternal fire, the raging fire, everlasting contempt, condemnation, and a variety of other descriptions.

Scholars agree that the nature of hell is the agony of being in the state of eternal exclusion and separation from God. The description of hell as a place of fire captures the reality of suffering and anguish apart from God. The rich man in Luke 16 was parched and thirsty because of the fiery environment. Is the fire literal or is it symbolic language? One scholar summed up the answer to the question in this way, "It is wiser to be concerned about escaping this eternal fire by true repentance than to engage in an unprofitable argument as to the nature of this fire" (Christian Dogmatics. Francis Pieper. Vol. 3, p. 546). The torment of hell described in the Bible is very real. Still, however, the subject of hell is very difficult to understand.

How can you get a grasp on final eternal separation from God? What perspective can you use? Typically, human beings use a perspective they can relate to. We reason that hell must be the worst thing ever. If that is true, it must resemble one of our worst experiences. Usually our worst experiences involve unjustified discomfort. When my family traveled home from Africa after a mission trip there, we experienced a span of about 14 hours during which we were stuck in a holding room at the airport in Bamako, Mali. The complete passenger load of a Boeing 767 was crammed into a small room with rows of broken-down blue metal seating units. We had access to two non-functioning bathrooms. We had no access to food or communication. The room was filled with cigarette smoke, the smell of jet exhaust, and everybody's two-day-old unwashed clothing. As human beings, we might compare that to hell. Some people in the room were doing just that! It was miserable. It was frustrating. And it was forced on us because airline workers decided to go on strike. No sleep, terrible smells, aching hunger, and the inability to communicate with loved ones: it added up to what many called hell.

Yet, there is much greater suffering endured by many. My uncle compared his experience on D-day during World War

father Abraham, but if someone from the dead goes to them, they will repent."

Notice the key facts of this hell case study. The person in hell is miserable, but he does not see his new existence as unfair. He does not ask questions about justice or express feelings of repentance. He continues on the same course he established during his life on earth: self-centered commands and control. The rich man didn't ask for a second chance. He didn't question God's planning. In fact, he wasn't even thinking about God. He never thought about God. Even in the midst of pain, he was thinking about how he could call the shots and how he could solve his own problems. Is hell unfair? A person in hell doesn't think so. Is hell too harsh? A person in hell is too busy being preoccupied with self to even think about punishment. Did God foul up His plan with the prospect of eternal torment? A hell dweller doesn't think about God or His plans. In other words, a person in hell doesn't have any of the objections we have about eternal punishment.

For further clarity, let's look at another case study. It is the Christmas story from Revelation chapter 12. The opening verses lead us to Mary, the birth of Jesus, and Satan's attempt to destroy the Savior:

> *A great and wondrous sign appeared in heaven: a woman clothed with the sun, with the moon under her feet and a crown of twelve stars on her head. She was pregnant and cried out in pain as she was about to give birth. Then another sign appeared in heaven: an enormous red dragon with seven heads and ten horns and seven crowns on his heads. His tail swept a third of the stars out of the sky and flung them to the earth. The*

dragon stood in front of the woman who was about to give birth, so that he might devour her child the moment it was born. She gave birth to a son, a male child, who will rule all the nations with an iron scepter. And her child was snatched up to God and to his throne (vss. 1-5).

In verse nine the dragon is identified as the devil. He and his angels were hurled down—the first residents of hell. They were defeated by the blood of the Lamb and by the word of witness to Jesus. This second case study, therefore, is an observation of the devil. What is the devil's attitude toward separation from God? Does Satan moan because he cannot have another chance and because he feels that the eternal fire option is much too harsh and completely unjust? Revelation 12 lets us know. Like the rich man, Satan wasn't even thinking about God. Verse twelve says about the devil: *"He is filled with fury, because he knows that his time is short."* Verse seventeen describes the church--all believers--as the woman. The verse says: *"Then the dragon was enraged at the woman and went off to make war against the rest of her offspring--those who obey God's commandments and hold to the testimony of Jesus."*

That is the heart of a hell dweller. There is no remorse or sense of unfairness. A hell dweller is at war with God, at odds with God, trying to be God. A hell dweller still craves command and control. A hell dweller knows that misery loves company. He wants to coerce everyone into suffering with him.

In his book The Case for Faith, Lee Strobel said, "Hell is not a place where people are consigned because they were pretty good blokes, but they just didn't believe the right stuff. They're consigned there, first and foremost, because they defy their maker and want to be at the center of the universe. Hell is not filled with people who have already repented, only God isn't gentle enough or good enough to let them out. It's filled with people who, for all eternity, still want to be the center of the universe and who persist in their God-defying rebellion" (p. 269).

Hell isn't unfair and it isn't too harsh--at least it isn't to the people who end up there. We grieve the possibility of seeing anyone enter eternal punishment. We desperately desire that no one would ever experience the fire of hell. We want grace and truth to prevail. And so does God. Remember, He desires that all people are saved and come to a knowledge of the truth (1 Timothy 2:4). As we study hell, we must never lose sight of the nature of God, His heart. Is hell bad planning on God's part? Is hell contrary to God's nature? Not at all. In fact, hell reinforces the nature of God's heart in a powerful way.

First, hell displays God's justice and comfort. For every person who has suffered persecution, pain, and abuse; for every victim of injustice and evil; hell shows that God does not overlook such sinful cruelty. On the contrary, all injustice, all evil, all deception, all impurity, all chaos, all death, and all hurt, will be conquered. Justice will be done. God is on His throne. He will come through for every hurting heart and soul. Hell shows that God will overcome and will punish evil. God cares about His children. He will not allow the injustice of victimizers to prevail.

Second, hell reveals God's deepest desire and motivation. The case study from Revelation shows this so well. That baby in the manger, the Savior Jesus, was the miraculous intervention of our loving Father God to bring us to Himself as

His redeemed children. He loved all people--the whole world-- and sent Jesus to die for all--including you! God's salvation effort revealed the real danger of our lives steeped in sin. We could be lost forever. The rebellion-based environment of hell loomed before sinful and broken humanity. The dragon's mouth was wide open. So God stepped in. It meant disowning His own Son. But God's heart yearns for you. He does not want you to be without Him and He does not want to spend eternity without you. In the Bible God pleads, *"I take no pleasure in the death of the wicked, but rather that they turn from their ways and live. Turn! Turn from your evil ways! Why will you die?" (Ezekiel 33:11)*

The teaching about hell in the Bible shows you what God doesn't want for you. He doesn't want you to perish. So, the Savior Jesus was born into our world, lived through each hour of what can be a very painful life, suffered insult and abuse, and finally died—more than that: He experienced hell, total separation from God, so you would never have to. Jesus cried out, *"My God, my God, why have you forsaken me?"* so those words would never have to pass your lips. Hell shows God's heart. It shows God's deepest desire and motivation: to save us from being lost forever and to spend eternity with us, His restored and redeemed people.

Finally, hell shows you how significant your life is to God. Think about it: God gave up everything because of His love for you and value of you. Jesus was not sent to this earth to save you from nothing. He wasn't born under the law to save you from fading into a neutral or reincarnated state. He didn't give up everything and take the form of a servant to save you from no consequence. No. Jesus came to rescue you from a horrible, unspeakable, and indescribably dreadful end: life without God. Jesus suffered real hell because your life has substance; it has meaning; it has an eternal purpose; it really matters. Even if your life is not everything you hope for right now, it is still completely precious to God. Hell reinforces that fact. The eternal stakes are high. Your life is irreplaceable. God was not about to lose you. Even if you can't grasp how significant and precious your life is, the crucified and risen Savior with His outstretched arms of forgiveness and new life tells you that God sees it that way. He says, "Trust me on this one. You mean everything to me." A real price was paid for you. That price was hell itself.

Hell fits into God's plan of righteousness and helps us understand His true nature. It also engages us with the urgency of God's work. There are many on earth who do not know Jesus as Savior. We are here to help them find out that they have hope. It's not necessary for death to have the last word. Jude 1:23 articulates the part we play in God's rescue work. The writer says, *"Snatch others from the fire and save them."* Real danger exists. Hell is real. We are here to help with God's efforts to save. The task is urgent and important.

Does this chapter mean that you have to like the prospect of hell? No. We share God's heart and pray that all people are saved. But we don't have to dismiss the idea of the existence of hell. We don't have to squirm when we encounter the Biblical teaching about eternal torment. We can acknowledge hell's reality and purpose as we trust that God knows what He is doing, that He stays consistent to His character and promises, and that even hell will work to His glory in the end.

Chapter Eight Questions for Thought and Discussion

1. Read Matthew 5:21-30. Find Jesus' references to hell and explain why He brought up the subject in this conversation with His followers.

2. How does Jesus' serious conversation about hell impact how seriously you take your obedience to Jesus and your resistance of careless sin and enticing temptation?

3. How do these references speak to those who deny hell's existence?

4. In what ways do verses 29-30 show Jesus' sincere care and concern for your life?

5. How do these verses clarify the importance of the Bible's teaching of hell?

6. Read Matthew 23:15, 33. How do these verses increase your understanding of God's justice in the face of evil?

7. Discuss how hell makes Jesus' death and our mission more meaningful and urgent?

Verse of God's Grace: Ephesians 2:8-9 *"For it is by grace you have been saved, through faith--and this not from yourselves, it is the gift of God--not by works, so that no one can boast."*

Note how you need to grow stronger in your walk with Jesus:

Jesus, the Afterlife, and You

"At his gate was laid a beggar named Lazarus, covered with sores and longing to eat what fell from the rich man's table. Even the dogs came and licked his sores."

Nine
Jesus, the Afterlife, and You

+

I started to write this book as I flew to a small town in Slovakia for a mission trip. As I pondered the subject of heaven, I realized that it could be compared to my flight in two very different ways. On one hand, heaven could be viewed as a person who sees an airplane flying overhead at 36,000 feet. It is a far away mystery, an otherworldly place to be speculated about and observed from a remote location. A study about heaven can become an out-of-this-world, highbrow, theological issue that we muse about and about which we formulate complex theological principles. On the other hand, heaven can be studied from the standpoint of a person in the airplane. Soaring at great heights on a personal journey, the person is "closer to heaven" than ever before. The view moves away from a theoretical and academic approach. It becomes very real and personal.

Most everyone who asks me about heaven does so out of a very deep and personal concern. Most of the time, random curiosity doesn't motivate the search for knowledge about heaven. A beloved brother, a precious wife, a child who died too soon—these are the points of motivation for the inquiries about heaven.

I've found that the quest for information about eternity is also motivated by the search for meaning and wholeness in life. A young man I met in Slovakia talked about his journey from the propaganda of Communism to the truth of Jesus Christ.

Communist teaching told him that he could do anything he put his mind and effort to. His ability and strength would take him far. This young man was on track to be a national soccer player. Suddenly, however, he became ill. A kidney ailment ended his soccer career. Almost overnight this strong and talented athlete realized that his strength and ability were very limited. Without the capacity to play soccer he felt empty and out of place in life. He tried yoga. He pursued more education. But he discovered that these were not the answers. Then he happened to attend a Bible class given by a friend and colleague. After hearing Jesus' words, this young man felt at home for the first time in his life. The Holy Spirit began to breathe new life into him. The grace of God began to renew him. Through the living Word of God, he became connected with the eternal. The young man found what he was looking for—more accurately, it found him!

The search in this man's life was truly a matter of life and death. He was engaging in the struggle that every person must face at one time or another. He was confronted with meaning versus meaninglessness, fulfillment versus emptiness. Eternal life was not a subject in school or dry reading material in dusty textbooks. It was not a theoretical quest or a casual subject for a Tuesday morning Bible study. For him, the subject of heaven, the prospect of eternal life, was a powerful confrontation with the question of his own destiny, the core meaning and purpose of his life. And God responded.

The Bible's teaching about heaven answers our big questions and addresses the significant needs we have. First, heaven provides comfort. Through Jesus' death on the cross and resurrection from the grave, the blessings of forgiveness and eternal life in heaven were poured into my friend's life. He was a new creation through the promise of the Word and through the miracle of Baptism. Jesus lived in him through the gift of Holy Communion. The gift of life was his. It was certain. It was paid in full.

The Bible's teaching about heaven is meant to bring you that great comfort. It is not included in the Bible to cause confusion and to perplex you with more questions. It's the simple truth of the Savior God sending His angels to carry you, like Lazarus, to Abraham's side. From the suffering of a sin-broken world, you, as a redeemed child of God, will be brought to a place of full restoration and wholeness. You can be assured that your loved ones who died in faith dwell in this wonderful place of complete peace and care. As St. Paul said about his proclamation of God's eternal plan: *"Therefore encourage each other with these words" (1 Thessalonians 4:18).* The comforting news of heaven sustains you as your heart aches for dear ones who have gone before you.

Second, heaven shows that God is truly in control. My Slovakian friend realized that God does have an eternal plan. Life does not depend on our strength, savvy, and strategizing. As our weaknesses and limitations loom before us, we are encouraged by the great eternal plan God reveals in the Scriptures. We can trust that God will bring everything together perfectly and wonderfully. When we get to heaven, we won't see a half-baked, poorly thought out strategy that overlooked a percentage of the world's need. We won't have to break the news to God that He really blew it. We will see that all things worked together for good. We will see that all things are bound together in Christ. We will see that God did better than we could ever ask for or imagine. He is in control. All will be well with our souls and with our loved ones, with our relationships and with our service, with the new creation and all who dwell there.

Third, the Bible's teaching about heaven gives us an urgent commission. My friend in Slovakia went from being a soccer player to studying for the ministry. When I met him, he was on his way to a doctorate in theology. But he wasn't lost in the academic world. His deep study of God's Word led him to help establish a Bible School that taught Christians how to reach out in a country that was recovering from Communist oppression. My friend knew that many people in his country didn't know Christ. So he acted on the urgent call and commission from God to help open the way to heaven for them.

One of the purposes of this book is to make you aware of that urgent call and commission of God. Knowledge about heaven, even loved ones in heaven, may be fulfilling. But God wants the knowledge of what happens when you die to fuel your ability to live for Him. Will YOU receive the gift of heaven that He gives? Will the place in heaven earned for you by His Son Jesus be YOURS? Will you hear the Word of God calling YOUR name? If so, will YOU reach out to people who have no idea about the gift of eternal life? Will you share the news that we have hope in this world because of Jesus? Will you help rescue people from a meaningless and empty life that leads only to eternal torment?

In Luke 16, Abraham told the rich man that everything needed for a person to get into heaven was available. The angels are ready to carry God's redeemed people to Abraham's side at just the right time. Will your 36,000-foot vantage point be a cold and academic look at heaven, or will you be on a meaningful and personal journey to the very heart of God?

In the third verse of the hymn "I am Jesus' Little Lamb," the author, Henrietta L. von Hayn, wrote words that reflected Jesus' description of Lazarus' wonderful journey to heaven:

> *Who so happy as I am, Even now the Shepherd's lamb?*
> *And when my short life is ended, By his angel host attended,*
> *He shall fold me to his breast, There within his arms to rest.*

That's a promise from Jesus who blesses you by graciously providing clear, comforting, and compelling news about what happens when you die.

Chapter Nine Questions for Thought and Discussion

1. Read 2 Peter 3:10-14. What urgency do these verses emphasize for life this side of heaven?

2. As verse 11 asks, what kind of person does this eternal urgency lead you to be?

3. Read Revelation 22:12-14. How do these verses motivate you to share the Good News of Jesus with others?

4. Who in your life right now needs to hear about Jesus and His gift of eternal life?

5. Read Romans 8:28-39. What do these verses tell you about God's plan and power?

6. How do these verses encourage you as you make your way toward heaven?

7. Read the parable of the rich man and Lazarus in Luke 16:19-31. Now that you've completed this book, what new insights, reasons for joy, questions, and confidence do you have about what happens when you die?

Verse of Jesus' Hope: John 11:25 *"I am the resurrection and the life. He who believes in me will live, even though he dies; and whoever lives and believes in me will never die."*

Note how this book has helped you grow in hope and understanding, and how it has helped heal your heart and soul:

About the Author

Michael Newman has served in ministry for over 20 years and continues to be active in writing, preaching, and teaching. At this time in his life he is thankful to be involved in developing missional communities in Texas. Married to his wife Cindy since 1983, they have been blessed with two wonderful daughters.

Check out these books written by Michael W. Newman:

STRUGGLE WELL
Living Through Life's Storms

REVELATION
What the Last Book of the Bible Really Means

SATAN'S LIES
Overcoming the Devil's Attempts to Stunt Your Spiritual Growth

STEPS FORWARD
The New Adventures of Ernest Thorpe

HARRISON TOWN
Discovering God's Grace in Bears, Prayers and County Fairs

For information and links to purchase books and e-books, go to **www.mnewman.org.**

Books are also available at Amazon.com or through your local Barnes and Noble bookseller.